There are not enough stars to r
heart of a Godly mother who lo
tears to my eyes and I cried.

As mother's, love regardless of w... .... g. ....g.. .. ..
them is unconditional. If you have lost a child or grandchild, sister, brother or
any loved one it hurts, but losing your child is a mother's pain that is deep. The
pain will always be there, but only God can give you his peace.

~ Carolyn Adams

A very poignant, touching, and honest revelation of what a grieving parent
feels. Truly a glimpse into the anguish and extreme pain and emptiness the loss
of a loved one brings. A must read for those dealing with the heartache of losing
a child.

~ Doris Thomas, Retired School Teacher

Wonderfully written, riveting, and heartfelt. For struggling Dads also.

~ Richard Weathersby

I would start reading and the tears started to flow. Then I would stop for a day,
start reading again, cry then smile. Your words as a mother and the words that
are in Calvin's voice flowing through you are so beautiful. I read them over and
over. I think you have expressed what I didn't have words for. I can say that I
found lines in every one of the poems/love letters that captured my heart and
my emotions.

~ Ardeth Sitt, Social Worker, LCSW

When your loved one has gone to be with the Lord, this is a beautiful treasure
that you will not want to miss reading. This is a "must have" book to assist you
on your journey with grief. These anointed poems will minister quietly and ever
so gently to your spirit.

This grieving mother's expression of sorrow and loss is countered with
encouragement and healing. Each time I have read through this book I have
experienced such a great peace in my spirit. I encourage you to not miss reading
this anointed book.

~ Pastor Mary Lu Saddoris

This book of poetry will bring you to tears, joy, hope, and peace. A very vulnerable and personal expressions of feelings; I could literally vision the agony she went through. There were times I could only read a chapter at a time because I was overwhelmed with my own emotions. I was so touched by each one of her poems. If you know of someone dealing with the loss of child or anyone, place a copy of this book in their hands.

~ Pastor Yvonne McCoy

Say Their Name is a very Real and Raw look into the life and heart of a mother whose grief, while paralyzing and almost debilitating at times, has taken her on a journey of reconnecting with her son. Though worlds apart, her love for her son somehow connects with him to tell a story of love that endures throughout eternity.

Through Wanda's gift of poetry, she is able to shed light on the grief process and allow those who have lost a child or a loved one to death, to heal and grow through it all; and even more, to know that they are still connected to their loved one by God's love.

~ Pastor Anitha Jones

Say Their Name is a scorchingly beautiful set of prayers and poems of what it is to love as a mother, to lose a beloved child, and to continue to forever love that child after they are gone. While I may never know what it is to lose a child, this book teaches how to begin to understand the never-ending state of grief, the heartfelt desire for parents to hear their child's name spoken out loud, that their child not be forgotten with the passage of time. It teaches how to be present for the bereaved parent—immediately after, throughout, and then long after the loss of their child. Ms. Weathersby's book is a perfect expression of a mother's pain after the loss of her beloved child– the shock, the inconsolable days and months and years of grief that follows. While they will grieve and hurt regardless, saying their child's name brings a taste of Godly sweetness and comfort that will momentarily cover the most devastating of losses one can survive.

~ Tina M. Moser, MLIS Access Services Librarian

Say Their Name

a mother's expression of
healing and love

by Wanda Weathersby

KINGDOM
PUBLISHING

Say Their Name

Published by Kingdom Publishing
PO Box 630443
Highlands Ranch, CO 80163
www.kingdom-publishing.com

Cover Design: Tracy Fagan
Select vector images courtesy of Vecteezy.com

ISBN 978-1-7333078-8-8 (print)

ISBN 978-1-7333078-9-5 (ebook)

Acknowledgments

*To my amazing family the Lilly's,
the Weathersby's, and the Curvin's,
that continues to be very supportive
and have stood by my side – I love you all.*

*To every parent that life has led them on a path
to the pain of child loss.*

*Nancy Jamerson, my friend, my editor.
Thank you for your encouragement, love and support
in completing this book. It is because of your encouragement these
poems are not in a drawer some place. Thanks Nancy for the hours
you spent with me on the phone, suggestions and honest feedback,
when you would read a poem and tell me there was more.*

*Your time spent on my behalf is
and has been truly priceless.*

Thank you Nancy!

My Husband

Thank you for being there through all the nights I've cried and couldn't sleep, for your love and support, and for never letting go of my hand.

Thank You!

Introduction

It is no accident you hold this book in your hands, written from my heart.

Either you have experienced this unexplainable pain or may know someone who has.

And either way - the life for a parent who has lost a child is forever altered.

You'll be alright a friend says, it's not about being alright I think to myself, it's about this feeling of emptiness, a feeling where something, actually someone, your child, my child is forever gone from this life. It's about how do I breathe and go through each day.

God has blessed me with a beautiful baby boy, and in my heart and mind it would be forever, at least till God calls me home. And for me, forever came much too soon.

As you read these poems know every word is heartfelt –

And thank you for taking a look inside the soul of a parent, who knows your heart, if this kind of pain has ever touched your life.

Table of Contents

Acknowledgments. iii

Introduction 1

Thanksgiving Day 6

The Pain That Will
    Always Be. 9

The Tears 10

God Still Sits On the Throne . . 14

Sleepless Nights 18

When the Night Falls. 20

Everyday 23

What I Wouldn't Give 24

The Dance 27

Appreciate the Times 30

Everyday It Hurts. 34

The Last Hug. 37

Smile. 38

I Scream 41

I Cry 42

When 46

Happy Birthday Mom 48

I Miss My Son. 50

My Heart Skips a Beat. 51

I Go Through the Motions . . . 52

You Are Always
    On My Mind 54

God Are You There 56

Mom I Want You to Live 58

GRIEF – What Is It. 61

Alive 66

Am I the Only Mother? 70

I am Okay –
    I Need You to Be 73

You Were a Good Mom
    to Me 74

One More Time 75

The Feathers – A Special Sign 77

I Just Feel Like. 78

Forever In My Heart 80

A Club I've Heard About 84

I Would Have Never Left
    Your Side. 88

I'll Never Get Over
    Missing You. 91

You See Me Smile. 92

Missing You 93

Take This Brick Off My Heart . 95

I Cry Inside 96

Life Is Not Life Without You. . . 97

My God Is Bigger 98

My Life 99

Say Their Name 102

Dedicated 107

Say Their Name

Wanda Weathersby

A

Glimpse

Into

My

Heart

Thanksgiving Day

Thoughts are racing through my mind
On Thanksgiving Day, what will I find
Heart racing, pounding as I travel a few hundred miles
My love one hasn't returned the phone call to me
Driving on a cold winter day
Snowing, icy roads, highway gate closed,
for all traffic to not go through
I ignore as I must get to you
What's this knot in my stomach I feel
Trusting God as this can't be real
It's Thanksgiving day, God don't make me sad
Thinking of you as a child and the fun we had
Well........
I'm here.....
I race to the door and turn the key
Rush to the bedroom, what will I see
I see you there on the floor,
I smile, my heart is calm for just a few seconds
I said:
"so glad you are alright
And I'm not upset you didn't return my calls,
just glad you are alright"

Then I reached out to touch you on the floor

And felt.........

Oh my God... ....

You are lifeless,

You are....... cold

And you are stiff

I just stare, I'm.... frozen like

And I had just thought for just a second, you were alright

God I should have been here, why wasn't I here....

Maybe I could have..... saved him.....

Run.......

Run.......

my mind tells me to run, with tears and disbelief

This can't be........

You're gone, really gone

From this place we call earth

And I must realize.......

From dust we all are and to dust we all will return

And now my heart broken, for you I will always yearn

Fresh in my mind this memory will be

That Thanksgiving Day, I found you taken from me.

Losing you........

A heartbreak

Like

None

Other

The Pain That Will Always Be

I have a pain cut deep inside my heart
It came the day in this world you did depart.
No longer do I try to explain the pain away
It greets me and is with me throughout each day.
Happy I am God gave you to me
My love for you will last throughout eternity.
Many good times I will cherish within
As the start of each day without you begins.
You are walking streets of gold
Yes standing tall and whole
Saying, Mom I now have the peace you prayed for me
As for the pain Mama, you feel will always be.
Just keep that love for me, yes mama,
Keep my love with you for all eternity,
I see the tears you cry late in the night
Mama just know each day you awake your child is alright.

The Tears

Yes I cry for you
In hopes to release this pain
I realize,
you have become heaven's gain.
I cry for you
as you are no longer here
yet in my mind,
I can hear you cheer,
Mom, I am okay
I want you to know
I love you very much Mom,
God has taken me through heaven's door
My family stood to meet me there
Embraced me with love
It filled the heaven's air
Yes I love you Mom, with all my heart
I am in heaven now,
with a brand new start.

Take care of my sisters and brothers

my nephews and nieces too

And always remember Mom,

to take care of you.

The tears will come

and I have seen you cry

Mom this is just so long

it is not goodbye.

Remember now

God gave me 36 years

And God is with you Mom,

and collects all your tears.

God knows your pain

and God knows your heart

God was with me, the day I did depart

So when you cry, listen to my cheers

And know, our God

is with you through the years.

Say Their Name

Wanda Weathersby

I

Will

Always

Love

You

God Still Sits On the Throne

The day came sooner than ever desired
that God called me home
You have to know Mom, even in death
God still sits on the throne
God came for me
and I know for me you grieve,
Even in this, keep trusting in God
and continue to believe
Heartbroken you are
I'm not here for you to see
Mom, I'm with the Father
Rejoicing for all eternity
If you could see me now and know
I've been made whole
I'm strolling with the Father
a wonderful sight to behold
Mom I have asked our Father
to heal you of your pain

To show you Mom

He's the God that still reigns

I would like you to know

You are never alone

And God is still God

And he still sits on the throne.

Right after the poem, God Still Sits On the Throne, was written, I went to the Bible on my cell phone and the scripture below was at the top of the screen:

I know the Lord is always with me,
I will not be shaken,
for He is right beside me

Psalms 16:8 NLT

Everytime

Someone has said the name

Of my son

Calvin

My heart leaps for joy

Sleepless Nights

God tell me how this could be
my beloved son no longer on earth with me
The pain that cuts deep seems too much for me,
tears roll down my cheek, I gently wipe away....
Because I know our hearts as mother and son
will reunite again someday.
Each day I look for you in a song that I hear
and I even hear your voice, as for me you do cheer
You say, "Mom I am okay, I am at peace
and I see the tears you cry
When you can't seem to sleep
I'd love to dry your eyes
And take your mind away,
from the day you found me without breath,
and you ran in disbelief
you ran from my death.

Wanda Weathersby

Mom my spirit lives on,

you are forever in my heart

Always

remember I was not alone

Jesus took my hand and led me to my new home.

And while things don't seem quite alright down there

I am near Mom, yes through those sleepless nights

And even on days,

when things don't quite seem quite right

Just know, I love you Mom, forever and always.

When the Night Falls

Thoughts racing through my mind
when you were here,
will I dream of you tonight,
will it be your voice I hear?
Lay my head on my pillow
the tears seem to fall,
realizing when the phone rings again
it won't be you to call.
Time is so precious
and quickly went away,
no warning to tell me
soon would be your last day.
Would I have clung to you more,
and never left your side?
Would I take your hand
and say, I love you?

When the night falls
my heart reminds me once again
you are no longer here,
and heaven is now your eternity.
When the night falls
I'm reminded this day
my beloved child
has really gone away,
To a place where there is no pain
Only peace, love and joy you have gained.
Your mother's heart
will never be the same
Each day I awake
to my heart of pain
My child, my child
a part of me you will forever be
And my love for you
shall last for all eternity
I realize never again will you call
and my heart so aches,
When the night falls.

Replaying

The Good Times

In My Mind

Over and Over

Again

Everyday

Everyday I awake without my child
telling myself I must go on
and my child is not here
Family photos never the same
holidays continue to remain
And I live with this pain
my child is not here
Still I look for signs
and at times I see
many things remind me of you
And the memories ever so close and near
and, still I go on
without my child
everyday.

What I Wouldn't Give

What I wouldn't give,
To talk to you again
To see you again
To hug you again
What I wouldn't give

What I wouldn't give,
To just hear your voice
To see your beautiful smile
To look into your eyes
What I wouldn't give

What I wouldn't give,
To just hold your hand
To sit and make future plans
To hear you say, I can
What I wouldn't give........

Wanda Weathersby

What I wouldn't give,

For you to be alive

To walk through the door

For just once more

What I wouldn't give

You took a part of me that day,

When you left and went away.

We didn't have a say,

What I wouldn't give

I'd give up everything I own,

To have you again return back home

What I wouldn't give

I loved you the day you were born

Watched you play the football games you won

I miss you everyday,

I'll love you for always

What I wouldn't give..........

Saying the name

Of those that have

Transitioned from this world

Is a treasure

The Dance

Today, I played your favorite song,
And asked you to dance with me
I stood and put my arms out
the way it use to be
And begin to sway from side to side,
feeling your presence ever so near
Laid my head on your shoulder
as tears begin to fall
Still moving from side to side,
with my telling you
How very much I love you
and how much I miss you
Surely, the warmth I felt that day,
was your way of telling me,
you love me still
The many things and times we shared
came rushing back to me
Wouldn't miss the chance to say
thank you my son, for this day
for, the dance.

Say Their Name

Strolling

With

The

Angels

Appreciate the Times

Appreciate the times with you,
Those times I thought I had so much more of
And the talks that would go on through the night
Appreciate the love you showed me,
Others knew you were proud I was your Mom

Appreciate the meals – going out to eat,
And you would share your future dreams
Seems it all came to an end one day,
When your spirit went away
You walked into the arms of Jesus,
What more could a mother ask
Just to know you are alright – and free at last
To know you are at peace
To know you have pain no more

Hard to accept, no more of your walking through the door -
And if I had the chance, to do it over again,
It would be to cherish the moments
Too quickly it came to an end
Appreciate the times with you
Yes, I always will
Just to know God gave you to me
And to thank God for the time you did live
I say just one more day,
And know – that would never be enough
Losing you at times seems unbearable
And truly extremely tough
And when I look around
At all that reminds me of you
I'll always keep you in my heart
And forever appreciate my time with you.

Say Their Name

"Tell'em I said

Rejoice

Tell'em I said

Rejoice

Tell'em I said

Rejoice"

My earthly father Rev. Oran Alton Lilly, spoke these words to me about 2 weeks before he transitioned from this world.

Everyone my daddy said, "Rejoice."

Everyday It Hurts

Hello World,

See this smile on my face

Behind it is pain and a mother's broken heart

Every day I awake,

Telling myself I did nothing wrong, sorry you are gone

My child lives on in my mind

Till the end of time

I cry – each day I cry

Was told the tears are healing

Life so precious – so short lived

Love you so much – what I wouldn't give

Dear Lord, I pray,

May I see my child in a dream,

So unreal it all seems

Strength from above,

Comes from my Lord and King

For you my child

these words I pen and sing

Wanda Weathersby

Sing of the joy

You brought into my life

Singing today, Yes, I truly miss your smile

Yes, it's been a while

Yes, I tell the world

Everyday it hurts

You're not here, for me to touch or feel

Seems so unreal

And yes, everyday it hurts.....

Visit

Me

In

My Dreams

Wanda Weathersby

The Last Hug

We stood in the dining room of your apartment,
You put your arm around me,
And said, "Thanks for coming Mom"
At that moment I remember
Being grateful for a hug from my son
So genuine, as you begin to shed a tear
At that moment I knew,
How much you love me
At that moment,
Time could have stood still
I keep the memories close to my heart
They will never part
From the first hug to the last
Forever embedded on my mind.

Smile

This smile on my face,

It comes with grace,

All by the grace of my God

Because behind this smile is pain

Seems a constant flow of rain

Since you've been gone

Since you've been gone,

Seems I have constant thoughts of you

And the things we use to do

I hear your voice in my mind

It seems all the time.

You say,

"Mom I'm really okay

Seems, I needed to go away

So, Mom, please don't cry

My leaving was not goodbye

I'll see you on the other side

I'll take your hand

Then you will understand

Until then..... Mom it's alright to, smile"

I'll be waiting for you

When it's your time

Mom, I am okay

Yes, I am okay

It's been a while –

Go ahead Mom and

Smile

My oldest daughter

brought a lemon cake

when she came to visit,

while my son's name

wasn't spoken verbally,

it was spoken to me

by her actions.

I Scream

I scream at the thought
of finding you without breath
And I scream because,
I couldn't bring you back
I scream silently,
And out loud sometimes
And I lay on the floor
And cry, ache, hurt
Still unbelievable in my mind,
Even with the passing of time
Still thank God
He gave you to me
I will love you for all eternity
Yes still......
I scream!

I Cry

I cry, when no one is looking
I cry late at night
I cry in my car
And when I'm walking,
by myself in a parking lot
I cry, when I go to the place,
Where you were laid to rest,
And when I walk to the mailbox
I sit down by the mailbox and cry.
I cry and think,
Surely, there are no more tears left
I cry at weddings,
And wish it were you getting married
And wish you were still here
I write poems about
this unexplainable pain
And yes, my beloved child
I cry.........

I

Miss

You

I really, really

Miss

You

Say Their Name

Wanda Weathersby

G
R
I
E
V
E

When

When do the tears stop
When does the pain end
Is this my life now
Without my child and friend
When will I awake
And God reveal to me,
You really are walking streets of gold
Just a glimpse I must see,
When will people not look at me strange
Or maybe it's just me
When will joy return
Will I be truly happy again
Or will this be my life
And I continue to pretend,
When is the pain not so intense
When will God send His angels to come to my defense

When will I know that I know

You my child – are truly with the Lord

Why must losing you be so very hard.

I have lost family before,

And I do recall the pain

Yet it seems within time

My God will stop this rain.

God has sent me signs before

To let me know you are alright

Why isn't that enough

Since you'll never return to my sight

So when God – when

Can you tell me when

That I know that I know,

My child is with You

And in a place,

where peace and love has no end.

Happy Birthday Mom

Mom it's okay to smile, it's okay to be happy
Hear from heaven this day,
Your child is at peace and my soul is at ease
So hear my heart I am asking you please
Singing songs of praise to you this day
Be sad no more and let me see you smile
Rest in my love, for being in heaven is beyond worthwhile
While you cry, when you laugh, and think of yesterday
I promise, my love for you has not gone away
So my dear Mom, be happy, and hear from heaven this day
My love is with you always and will never go away
I love you Mom, on earth
I love you in heaven
And absent in body I love you still
Yes, I always will
Hear me say, to you this day
Happy Birthday Mom.

Wanda Weathersby

My youngest daughter
made me a lemon cake
for my birthday
and she bought yellow balloons
and yellow decorations.
Lemon cake was my son's
favorite cake and
the last cake I made for him.

I Miss My Son

I miss your smile, I miss your touch
God knows I miss you so very much
I miss the times, we would sit and laugh
Those times that went much too fast
I miss your saying goodnight I love you Mom
I miss the times of watching TV
The times you hugged and thanked me
It's the simple things, I miss going out to eat
I miss just your time with me
I miss the phone ringing late at night
Just to hear your voice, and know all was once alright
Yes, yes, I miss my son

My Heart Skips a Beat

My heart skips a beat and no one can see
There's a beat for you and a beat for me
It will stay that way from now until,
Till we meet again and my heart will heal
From the pain of losing you here
On this earth, still feel you near
Never knew someone could think so much of another
It happens without effort my thinking of you
Going through the motions as each day I get through
I wake up and say morning to you
Thankful you ran this race and won
You've gone a path we will all cross someday
Came sooner for you as I had no say
Yes, my heart skips a beat, as it now beats for two
Until I have joined hands again someday with you.

I Go Through the Motions

I go through the motions, each and every day

No one seems to notice

The pain has not gone away

I remind myself I'm still among the living

And with God's love in me, I keep on giving

Yes, I give of my time and encourage a few

Each day I awake, I still say hello to you

I scream in my car and cry in the shower

My mind goes back to the day that very hour

That a plug was pulled and I became weak without power

Yes, I shall go on and I'm missing you

I just go through the motions

and do what I need to

Listen, I go through the motions.....

My middle daughter

and

My daughter-in-law

A pillar of strength

Thank You

You Are Always On My Mind

When I wake up I find myself thinking of you

Remembering the things we use to do

As I go through my day I see your face

It seems a thousand times

And I can't deny, you're always on my mind

So many pictures to remind me of you

Of you growing up, till I said good bye to you

Except it's not goodbye, it's really so long

One day I'll join you and heaven will also be my home

Since you went away still find it hard to believe

You are no longer here for me to see

Since you went away, my world now is upside down

Missing those times of laughter and having you around

And those many trips driving around town

So I go through each day thinking of you along the way

You are always on my mind

And will remain that way forever

Even now and till the end of time

Today

I

Cried

God Are You There

God it's me, are you there?
You must have known the deep pain this would cause
Did I do something wrong to have my son leave
Day after day – my heart still grieves
Surely God you have a few tubs of my tears by now
And each day when I feel there are no more tears,
they come again
I look around at all the happy people
and my heart is broken
Why I ask why myself, surely other mothers
May have asked the same
Stop trying to analyze your child passing
I say in my mind
Do you believe the day he left was his time
Hold on to your memories
And cherish your times together
Your son will always be your son
And you will always be his mother

God are you there, yes I question why
Why did it seem my child needed to die
And
God said, "weep for I know you will,
I haven't left your side I'll be your guide."
"God are you there, you ask
I am, I am all seeing, all knowing
Yes I am, I am everywhere
Yes, even now, in your pain
I am there, I am, I am everywhere
I was with your child, when your child left this world
Yes, I was there
I am,
I am everywhere."

Mom I Want You to Live

Mom my time on earth is done
I have a request for you
To live out your life for your son
I watch you each day
And you knowing I've gone away
The tears come as they may
Live your life Mom, is what I have to say
Your son is in a good place
Spending time with Jesus
A reason for you to smile
We each will one day walk our last mile
Mom, I know you miss me
And I know you always will
You my mother have been summoned
To get out and live
Do the things that once brought you joy
And know my spirit is with you always

As you go through your day and enjoy

Just got to see that smile on my Mama's face once again

Keep reaching Mom

As you reach out your hand to lend

lend your smile, lend your joy and peace

And know as I walk around heaven, I am having a feast

Yes, Mom your son has gone away

We'll meet on the other side one day

So Mom for me – go ahead and live

You still have much within you to give

Yes Mom I love you

And I always will.

Another

Day

Without

You

GRIEF – What Is It

What is grief?

It's the thing that breaks your heart in a million pieces

It makes you cry even in times you think you are doing alright

It makes you scream when you are in your car alone

Grief – what is grief?

It's a pain that has hit me to my core

It's the shock that hits you more

You know when a loved one leaves

Your mother, father, sister, brother

And yes, your child

It brings you to your knees and steals and takes away your joy

Grief – what is it?

It's what at times mere words could not explain your pain

It's what you want to be a bad dream and to go away

It's a very unwelcomed time in one's life

It makes you scream and want to hit things

As if that would cause the pain to subside

Grief, what is it?

It's an everyday battle of a loved one lost

It's missing them

And still loving them although they are gone

Grief, what is it?

It's my stomach wrapped in knots

It's my own denial

Sitting at a memorial for the funeral service

It's the worst pain

It's believing and knowing

You will see your loved one again.

Grief, what is it?

It reminds you of missed opportunities

Words never spoken

It's me today –

Writing this with a broken heart

Grief, what is it?

I believe you may know

It greets me

It surrounds me

It tries to consume me

Grief – what is it?

It's still trusting in God

When the pain is so deep

It's hurting beyond belief

Yes to me my friend, that is grief

Yes grief..........

What is it..........

FAMILY

**Texas, Oklahoma, Colorado
Florida, Arkansas, Pennsylvania
California, Michigan, Washington state
and Illinois**

You came through

THANK YOU!

Woman of God

Great wisdom

Thanks Mom

I'll Forever

Love and Miss you!

Alive

Alive – everyone I see is alive

Laughing, smiling, playing, having a wonderful time

And my child is......

"Mom, listen to me,
I am more alive now than I've ever been
I'm free to sing
I'm free to dance
I'm free to write poetry
Mom, I'm free from a world full of sin
Free from the pain, the hurt,
Mom, so much more I have gained"
Life anew
Life beyond what you see
A life where your child is truly free
Mom I'm alive soaring with the angels
Yes Mom, I'm free
I soar with the angels
I am alive in a place beyond earth
I'm alive!
I'm not there for you to see
I live for all eternity.
Yes Mom, I'm free!"

Say Their Name

Say Their Name
Remember them on
Birthdays
Holidays
Transition days
Family Reunions
Yes remember them
with a phone call
a text
a handwritten note
And just remember to,
Say Their Name.

Am I the Only Mother?

Am I the only mother that cries in this pain?

Stand still in the rain

To think, what I could have done

While I know not to blame, to not feel ashamed

That God said "no" to my prayer

To press on and pray,

Is this now my new way?

To live out my days

To feel blessed for the time

No matter how short or how long

To write out a song of my pain

I stand in the rain

I stand in this pain

Knowing God hasn't left my side

I will go on, as I write this song

My child would have it no other way

Wanda Weathersby

Am I the only mother?

To get under the cover and cry

To someday stop asking why

Going on, moving forward, my life forever changed

The pain remains,

So I ask,

Am I the only mother......

Grieving......

No Time Limit

Wanda Weathersby

I am Okay – I Need You to Be

I am okay my son,
I'm just not wonderful, great, or marvelous
Those are the things I once was before you left

Mom, the hole in your heart will always be
Think about with Christ I spend eternity
Think about the fun times we shared
The joy you bring to others and how much you always cared
Yes, Mom I am okay
And I need you to be.

You Were a Good Mom to Me

My dear mother, you must not blame *yourself*,
For what has happened to me,
And this I know is true
I made choices that were not always best for me
I know Mom; you would have saved me from the pain
It was a decision; I made to step out in the rain
You my dear mother, you did all you knew to do
You love me Mom and this I know is true
What I've searched for I have found
I am near, my spirit is always around
Mom, *You Were* a Good Mom to me.

One More Time

Just thought I'd see you once again
Just thought I'd see you one more time
I really wanna see you
I really wanna see you
One more time.

Why did you have to leave me
Why did you have to go
Why couldn't you stay a little longer
You know I miss you so
You know I miss you so

Just thought I'd see you one more time.

A

Love

That

Never

Ends

The Feathers – A Special Sign

I woke up this morning and it was almost like any other day, except you're not here. You're forever 36. I missed you yesterday, I miss you today, I'll miss you tomorrow, and I'll miss you for always. Starting my day like I always do, thinking of and journaling to you.

I finish and toss my journal on the night stand, then finish the rest of my morning routine. I head for a relaxing shower in the tiny bathroom aboard the ship. I pull off my nightcap, and it seems out of nowhere a feather floats down, I gasp and silently cry.

You see, feathers remind me of you, my handsome son.

In awe, my heart sings and there are more tears. My clothes for the morning are draped over the chair in the stateroom of the cabin. I remove my shirt off the chair and there was, another feather.

I am truly amazed.

This time I smile; thank God and say, "Hi Calvin, I had a tough day yesterday; January 2nd is your birthday."

Around 3:30 pm I decide to indulge in another one of my daily routines. I head for the workout room, suddenly I'm stopped in my tracks as there in the hallway is another feather. Yes, a third feather. My heart smiles.

Impulsively, before returning to the cabin, I decide to stop by the jewelry store. As I enter the store, I see a young lady and written on her shirt is the name Calvin, well Calvin Klein actually; however, it was the name Calvin that caught my eye.

I'm smiling again because she's wearing a shirt with the name Calvin in bold letters on the front. I feel peace within me.

I make it back to the cabin to get ready for dinner aboard the ship which is always an adventure. Before I walk out the door of the cabin, I look down and right at the door was a fourth feather lying on the floor. My heart sings even more.

Thank you, God, for the signs today.

It is then I remember something my beloved brother Alton would often say to me, "Wanda, look for the signs. Life gives us many signs." I am forever grateful for the signs on January 3rd. My brother is right, signs… they are all around us.

I Just Feel Like

I just feel like I didn't get the chance to say goodbye
So grateful for all the good times we had
Your leaving has made me so very sad
I just feel like I didn't get the chance to say goodbye
The last hug, was just that, the last hug
The last time we went to eat together was the last
The last time we walked around the mall, was the last
We did not know those times were the last times
And I say,
So long, see you on the other side
And I just feel like...........

Wanda Weathersby

I am grateful

For my child, God gave to me

I am grateful for

Our time together

On this earth

Forever In My Heart

My beloved child
You are forever in my heart and always will be
From now and throughout eternity
A day does not go by I don't have thoughts of you,
Of all the good times and the things we use to do.
I awake each day knowing, on earth you are no longer here
And soon I hear your voice in my mind
And I hear you as you cheer.

Mom I'd wipe the tears if I could
You must know I'm always near
I see you when you start each day
And when you walk along the way
One thing for certain and Mom you must know
My love for you is stronger than ever before
Seems I needed to go

Hold on my dear mother to so very much we shared

For many others, I saw you reach out and how you cared.

So Mother's Day is approaching and you will be without your son

In this life we all have a race to run, so very glad I've won.

For my new life in heaven, has only just begun

Weep for me Mom, as for you it's a must,

Just remember our body is only dust

So when you awake, and I'm not physically there, you know I did depart

I know, that I know, I'll forever be in my mother's heart.

Say Their Name

Time......

Our time.....

Much too brief

A Club I've Heard About

I've joined a club I've heard about
A club I never dreamed I would be a part of
Met some amazing women along the way
Sharing a common bond now as we each recall the day
Our lives forever changed
And our love forever remain
In her eyes, I recognize the pain
That cuts to the core of our being
I understand her tears
No matter the number of years
A beat of our heart has gone away,
Holidays, birthdays never the same
The empty space forever remains,
The life we knew will not be the same
A glimpse of joy here and there
Life so different and it doesn't seem fair
This grief doesn't leave with time
Will forever miss this child of mine
He has crossed over to the other side

The pain I feel sometimes I don't hide

Forever, grateful Jesus was his guide

Understand when I mention my child's name

A reason for my heart to smile

It's the love between a mother and child

Makes living this life worthwhile.

Parents remember John 3:16,

To remind you God has your king or queen

Yes, my heart is broken, this hurt doesn't mend,

With me now and will be till my end

Mothers / Fathers we realize each and every day

Our beloved child has gone away.

And yes, I realize,

I've now joined a club, I heard about.

Say Their Name

SiS Group
Sisters in Solace

What Love, yes what love
We have for each other
Can't thank you enough
For the love and support
Remembering our times
the talks, the laughter, the tears
How we talk so openly, so freely
From one heart to another
As we share this unexplainable pain.....

I Would Have Never Left Your Side

I would have never left your side
I would have saved you if I could
I would hold on to every moment as any mother would
I would think of all the things I needed to say, before you went away
Listened one more time to hear your voice, if I only had the chance
You'd be here on earth with me, making plans for days ahead
Things left undone remain undone
Dreams seem to stop in the tracks,
Why does it hurt so very much to see you go
Why didn't I know, time was so short
So today I told a young lady,
Not speaking to her Mom
She is wasting precious time in closing the door
On the woman, who gave her life
My prayer for that mother and child, God help them end their strife
Life's too short not to love
Life is too short to hold on to words that hurt us yesterday
Because tomorrow is not promised we will stay

Wanda Weathersby

My heart bleeds that you are gone
Keep telling myself to go on
Go on in this pain, standing in the rain.
Just know my child
I would have never left your side.

My loved one

Your loved one

Will always live on in our hearts

And in our minds

Even till the end of time

I'll Never Get Over Missing You

I woke up this morning with you on my mind
Then I realize it will be this way all the time
I go through my day and still my heart aches
Etched in my mind when you left this world
Will always remember the date
Start each day with a prayer and reading the Word
Pray for those of us still here as we go on each day
Going on without you, still feel the pain
Seems to be no way to stop this rain
Tears do flow and I question why
You are no longer here and still I cry
So this morning, I realize how much I am missing you
And clearly always understand
I'll never get over missing you.

You See Me Smile

You see me smile and it looks like I've gone on with my life,
I've learned to hide the pain, the world would not understand
My hidden pain from this loss cuts deep,
And each day I continue to weep.
And the world, you see me smile,
Each day God gives me breath and I'm still here
In my mind, I hear my child speak
His spirit brings me comfort even when I weep.
He's not here and yes world you see me smile,
You see me smile............

Wanda Weathersby

Missing You

Miss your smile and the way we use to talk,
Miss the days we took those walks.
Miss the meals we shared and we had our laughs,
As we each worked in the kitchen having our tasks
Miss the joy we shared as mother and son
And watching your life, grow into a blessed one
So grateful, it is not goodbye and I'll see you again,
Heaven is big enough for us and all our family and friends
Each day I think of you and know I always will
My love for my child, I will forever feel
So when my mind wonders, and I seem sad or blue
I know, that I know
I'll always be missing you!

**At my oldest brother's funeral
I was asked to say a prayer.
For some reason I'll always
Remember these words,
I prayed**

**"God you could have given us more
and you could have given us less –
Thank you Father
Thank you
For the time you gave to us."**

Wanda Weathersby

Take This Brick Off My Heart

Take this brick off my heart, it's really crushing me
Take this brick off my heart, having trouble breathing
This pain is weighing on me; I'm told it will always be
Just take this brick off my heart
So, that I can breathe

I Cry Inside

I cry inside now, and the tears are from my heart

The truth is my child has left this world

And that is when the pain did start

I cry inside to hide my tears

To release the inner and outside fears

I cry inside, as it keeps those tears hidden from the world

As I lay in bed, at times and bring my body to a curl position,

I cry inside, as that's a hidden part of me

And I realize, no one can see, not even those closest to me

Yes, I cry inside......

Wanda Weathersby

Life Is Not Life Without You

Life is not life without you,
I'm alive – I'm breathing
Moving it seems
Still, life is not life without you.
I go on because I'm here,
Seems no longer anything to fear,
As life is not life without you........

My God Is Bigger

My God is bigger than the death that took my child much too soon

God is bigger than the sun, the stars and the moon

God is bigger than the pain that at times have consumed me

My God is bigger than we could ever imagine

One day at a time my God gets me through

Help us all Lord that have lost a child

Stay with us even when one day we walk our last mile,

Death, oh death, where is your sting

My God, my Savior, steps in the ring

He lifts me up and gives my soul peace

Calms my mind puts me at ease

Been through much and yes I trust Him

Even in times when things look dim

My God is bigger, and I will always trust Him.

Wanda Weathersby

My Life

My life doesn't seem like my life anymore,
I'm awake – I go through the motions
I stay busy, keep moving I say
And oh the hidden pain,
I smile – where has my joy gone
Tears fill my eyes
A friend asks, what's wrong
What's wrong I think,
Family pictures will never be the same
I smile when I hear your name
My life has changed, it's shifted
Shifted to a place – where my heart does not feel whole
I'll see you again,
And it's then – complete joy is restored
And oh, my life.......

Wanda Weathersby

1 Corinthians 13:13

Say Their Name

Will you say their name?
They are always on our mind
Until the end of time

You think it might bother me
When it really brings me joy

Will you say their name?
They are always on our mind
Even until the end of time

Share some fun times you had
It will really make me glad

Will you say their name?
They are always on our mind
Even till the end of time

Wanda Weathersby

When is the right time you say?
It can be now or it can be any day

Will you say their name?
They are always on our mind
Even until the end of time

It lets me know you remember
Just how much my loved one means to me

Will you say their name?
They are always on our mind
Yes, even till the end of time....

I have found myself, standing in the rain
Feeling this pain
One request
Just say their name....

I

Think of you

Everyday

Always have

Always will

Dedicated

To My Son

Calvin Chester Curvin

January 2, 1980 – November 24, 2016

About the Author

Wanda has enjoyed expressing herself through words for many years. After receiving many accolades for her poetry and learning of the impact her poems had on other parents going through the grief of the loss of a child, she was encouraged to share her work in honor of her son Calvin. Through the unexpected loss of her beloved son Calvin, she learned to trust God even more in the storms of life. She recently relocated to Florida where she lives with her loving husband Ric. When Wanda is not writing poetry she is exercising, encouraging those she encounters, and enjoying traveling.

One Last Thing…

If this book has touched your heart, given you hope, or given you a sense of peace and comfort, please take a moment to write a review. Please visit any **online bookstore** or **GoodReads.com**, search for this book and tell others about your experience. It would also be an honor if you share this resource on any of your social media pages.

Your review does make a difference in helping others find this resource.

CPSIA information can be obtained
at www.ICGtesting.com
Printed in the USA
JSHW021942170722
28205JS00002B/139